VITAMIN
RICH

TIGER BOOKS INTERNATIONAL
LONDON

2439
This edition published 1993 by Tiger Books International PLC, London
© 1991 Coombe Books
ISBN 1-85501-311-8

Introduction

Vitamins are substances that are vital to the maintenance of our bodies, yet so much is written concerning these invisible, potent elements in our food that few of us can tell fact from fiction.

There are many different vitamins, but we only need each in very small quantities, and if we maintain a well balanced and varied diet, the food we eat will generally provide us with more than enough vitamins for our daily needs. In certain circumstances, however, such as during pregnancy, illness or in old age, vitamin supplements may be required, and in these cases professional advice should be sought.

Vitamins are mainly identified by letter, but this in no way indicates their order of importance. In the case of vitamin B, there are several complex variations of vitamins within the one heading, and this is called the 'B complex'. The table below gives general guidance on some of the main vitamins, their source and function.

VITAMIN	SOURCE	FUNCTION
A	Oily fish, fats, offal, carrots, green vegetables, tomatoes, watercress	General growth, good eyesight, healthy skin
B.1	Yeast extract, wheatgerm, peanuts, wholemeal bread, eggs, pulses	Assists the nervous system and metabolism. Is water soluble and therefore easily lost in cooking
B.2	Milk, dairy products, almonds, mushrooms, pulses, red meat, green vegetables	Assists the metabolism and maintains health of mouth, lips and skin
B.3	Milk, eggs, yeast extract, red meat, dried apricots	Essential to the nervous system
B.6	Yeast, whole cereal products, offal, dairy products, bananas, leaf vegetables	Helps production of new cells and promotes nervous health
B.12	Offal, meat, eggs, cheese, milk	Assists the production of red blood cells
C	Fruit and vegetables	Helps the body resist infection, promotes good skin, helps absorption of iron
D	Oily fish, fats, dairy products, offal, red meat	Helps promote strong bones and teeth. Is produced in the body when there is exposure to sunlight
E	Whole cereal products, eggs, nuts, vegetable oil and wholemeal flour	Necessary for upkeep of blood cells, tissues and membranes
K	Widely available in many foods such as green vegetables, eggs and cereals	Helps blood to clot and assists in the healing of wounds

SERVES 6-8

COUNTRYSIDE TERRINE

This impressive terrine looks very professional yet is simple to make.

450g/1lb pig liver, minced
340g/12oz lean pork, minced
225g/8oz pork sausagemeat
1 clove garlic, crushed
2 shallots, finely chopped
45ml/3 tbsps Cognac
2.5ml/½ tsp ground allspice
Salt and freshly ground black pepper
5ml/1 tsp chopped fresh thyme or sage
225g/8oz streaky bacon, rind and any bones removed
30ml/2 tbsps double cream
120g/4oz smoked tongue or ham, cut into 6mm/¼-inch cubes
1 large bay leaf

1. Preheat oven to 180°C/350°F/Gas Mark 4.

2. In a large bowl, mix together the minced liver and pork, sausagemeat, garlic, shallots, Cognac, allspice, salt, pepper, and thyme. Stir with a wooden spoon until the ingredients are evenly mixed, but still coarse in texture.

3. Lay the strips of bacon on a flat surface and stretch them with the back of a knife.

4. Line a 900g/2lb loaf dish evenly with the strips of bacon, overlapping each strip slightly to avoid any of the terrine mixture pushing through during cooking.

5. Add the cream, cubed tongue and ham to the liver and pork mixture, blending with your hands to keep the texture coarse.

6. Press the terrine mixture into the bacon-lined loaf dish, spreading it evenly, and pushing down lightly to remove any air bubbles.

7. Place the bay leaf on the top and fold over any overlapping edges of bacon.

8. Cover the dish with a tight-fitting lid or two layers of aluminium foil.

9. Stand the loaf dish in a roasting tin and pour enough water around it to come halfway up the sides of the dish.

10. Bake the terrine for 2 hours, or until the juices run clear when a knife is inserted into the centre.

11. Remove the lid or foil and replace this with some fresh foil.

12. Weigh down the terrine with cans of food or balance scale weights. Allow the terrine to cool at room temperature, then refrigerate it overnight if possible, still weighted, until it is completely chilled and firm.

13. To serve, remove the weights and foil and carefully turn the terrine out onto a serving plate. Scrape away any fat or jelly that may be on the outside of the terrine, and cut into slices just before serving.

Step 4 Line a 900g/2lb loaf tin evenly with the strips of bacon, overlapping each strip slightly.

Step 12 Cover the terrine with a double thickness of fresh foil and weight it down with cans or scale weights.

Cook's Notes

Time
Preparation takes about 25 minutes, plus refrigeration time. Cooking takes approximately 2 hours.

Freezing
This recipe will freeze well for up to 3 months. It should be packed in plastic wrap and not aluminium or metal foil.

Vitamin Content
This recipe is an extremely good source of all the B complex vitamins.

SERVES 4

TARAMASALATA

This well known, classic Greek starter is a delicious way of improving your intake of vitamins B and C.

90g/3oz smoked cod roe
6 slices white bread, crusts removed
1 lemon
1 small onion, finely chopped
90ml/6 tbsps olive oil
Black olives and chopped fresh parsley, for garnish

1. Cut the cod roe in half and scrape out the centre into a bowl. Discard the skin.

Step 1 Cut the cods roe in half and carefully remove the soft insides using a small spoon. Discard the skin.

Step 2 Squeeze the soaked bread to remove the excess moisture.

Step 5 Gradually add the oil to the fish mixture, beating continuously and very vigorously between additions to prevent curdling.

2. Put the bread into a bowl along with ¼ pint warm water. Allow the bread to soak for about 10 minutes, then drain off the water and squeeze the bread until it is almost dry. Add the bread to the bowl containing the cod roe.

3. Squeeze the lemon and add the juice to the bread and roe, stirring it well.

4. Put the cod roe mixture into a blender or food processor, along with the onion. Process until the ingredients form a smooth paste.

5. Return the blended cod roe mixture to a bowl and gradually beat in the oil, a little at a time, as if making mayonnaise. Beat the mixture very thoroughly between additions with a whisk or wooden spoon.

6. Refrigerate the taramasalata for at least ½ hour to chill thoroughly.

7. Transfer the mixture to a serving bowl and garnish with the black olives and chopped parsley.

Cook's Notes

Time
Preparation takes about 15-25 minutes, plus refrigeration time.

Cook's Tip
Prepare the taramasalata in advance, but remove it from the refrigerator 20 minutes before serving.

Serving Idea
Warm pitta breads and toasts, cut into fingers and used for dipping, make an excellent accompaniment.

Watchpoint
Do not add the oil too quickly or the mixture will curdle. If it does, add a little more soaked bread to draw it back together again.

Vitamin Content
Vitamin B complex and also vitamin C.

SERVES 4
WATERCRESS SOUP

Watercress is packed with vitamins A, C and K, and makes delicious soup.

60g/2oz butter
1 leek, cleaned and thinly sliced
225g/8oz potatoes, peeled and sliced thinly
570ml/1 pint chicken stock
Pinch grated nutmeg
Salt and freshly ground black pepper
4 good bunches of watercress, washed and trimmed
45ml/3 tbsps cream
Few extra sprigs of watercress for garnish

1. Melt the butter in a large saucepan and gently cook the leek until it is just soft, stirring frequently to prevent it from browning.

2. Add the potatoes, stock, nutmeg and seasoning to the saucepan. Bring to the boil, then cover and simmer for 15 minutes.

3. Add the watercress and simmer for a further 10 minutes.

4. Cool the soup slightly, then using a food processor or blender, process until the vegetables are very finely chopped. Rinse the saucepan and stand a fine meshed sieve over the cleaned pan.

5. Push the puréed soup through the sieve using the back of a wooden spoon, working the watercress and vegetables through the mesh until only the tough stalks remain and the soup in the pan is a fine purée.

6. Adjust the seasoning and stir the cream into the soup. Reheat gently, taking care not to boil it. Serve garnished with the reserved watercress sprigs and a little cream if desired.

Step 1 Slowly soften the leek in the melted butter, stirring to prevent it from browning.

Step 4 Blend the soup in a food processor or liquidiser until the vegetables are very finely chopped.

Step 5 Push the soup through a fine meshed sieve using a wooden spoon, work the vegetable pulp through until only the tough stalks remain in the sieve.

Cook's Notes

Time
Preparation takes 15 minutes, cooking takes about 45 minutes.

Serving Idea
Chill the soup, and serve on a bed of crushed ice for a delicious variation.

Vitamin Content
Watercress is an excellent source of vitamins A, C and K.

SERVES 4

GAZPACHO

*Gazpacho is a typically Spanish soup which is served well chilled,
accompanied by a selection of fresh vegetables.*

450g/1lb ripe tomatoes
1 onion, peeled and chopped
1 green pepper, seeded and diced
½ cucumber, chopped
30ml/2 tbsps stale white breadcrumbs
2 cloves garlic, crushed
30ml/2 tbsps red wine vinegar
570ml/1 pint tomato juice
Salt and freshly ground black pepper

Accompaniments
½ cucumber, diced
10 spring onions, chopped
225g/8oz tomatoes, skinned, seeded and chopped
1 large green pepper, seeded and diced

1. Cut a small cross in the top of each of the ripe tomatoes, and plunge into a bowl of boiling water for a few seconds.

2. Carefully peel the skin away from the blanched tomatoes. Discard the skin and roughly chop the tomatoes, removing the tough stalk as you do.

3. Put the roughly chopped tomatoes into a liquidiser or food processor, along with the onion, pepper and cucumber. Blend until finely chopped.

4. Put the chopped vegetables into a bowl with the breadcrumbs, garlic, vinegar and tomato juice. Mix well to blend evenly and allow to stand for 15 minutes.

5. Season the tomato soup thoroughly, then push through a fine meshed sieve using the back of a wooden spoon and working well to press all the vegetables through, but keeping the pips out of the resulting purée.

6. Chill the soup well before serving, surrounded by bowls containing the accompaniments.

Step 2 Carefully peel the skin away from the blanched tomatoes using a sharp knife.

Step 5 Push the puréed vegetables through a nylon sieve using the back of a wooden spoon, working until all the pulp has been pressed through and the tomato pips remain.

Cook's Notes

Time
Preparation takes approximately 20 minutes, plus chilling time.

Serving Idea
Serve the individual bowls of soup on crushed ice.

Freezing
This soup is ideal for freezing.

Vitamin Content
Extremely high in vitamin C and the tomatoes are a good source of vitamin A.

SERVES 4

MUSSEL SOUP

*Shellfish contain a multitude of vitamins and minerals, especially vitamins A,
E, D and K, and this soup is, therefore, a delicious way of making sure you
have a good supply of all of these.*

2 lts/4 pints fresh mussels
60g/2oz butter
2 onions, peeled and finely chopped
2 cloves garlic, crushed
280ml/½ pint dry white wine
280ml/½ pint water
30ml/2 tbsps lemon juice
60g/2oz fresh white breadcrumbs
30ml/2 tbsps freshly chopped parsley
Salt and freshly ground black pepper

1. Scrub the mussels with a stiff brush and remove any barnacle shells or pieces of seaweed that are attached to them.

2. Tap each mussel sharply to make sure that it closes tightly.

3. Melt the butter in a large saucepan and gently fry the onions and garlic until they are soft, but not browned.

4. Add the mussels, wine, water and lemon juice to the pan, and bring to the boil. Season with salt and pepper,

then cover and cook for approximately 10 minutes or until all the mussel shells have completely opened.

5. Discard any mussels which have not opened fully.

6. Strain the mussels through a colander and return the juices and stock to the saucepan. Put the mussels in a serving tureen and keep warm.

7. Add the breadcrumbs and the parsley to the mussel juices and bring them to the boil. Adjust the seasoning, and serve over the mussels in the tureen. Serve immediately.

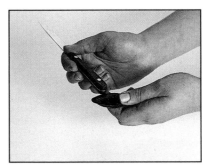

Step 2 Tap each mussel sharply with the handle of a knife to make sure that they shut tightly. Discard any that do not.

Step 1 Scrub the mussels with a stiff brush, removing any barnacles and pieces of seaweed which may be attached to the shells.

Step 4 Cook the mussels until they have all completely opened. Discard any that remain closed.

Cook's Notes

Time
Preparation takes 15 minutes, cooking takes approximately 20 minutes.

Watchpoint
When cooking fresh mussels, great care must be taken to ensure that they are safe to eat. Discard any that do not shut tightly before cooking, or do not open after cooking.

Serving Idea
Serve with warm French bread.

Vitamin Content
This soup contains vitamins A, B, E and K.

SERVES 4-6

SPINACH GNOCCHI

Gnocchi are delicious spinach and cheese dumplings which can be served as a healthy starter or snack.

120g/4oz chopped, frozen spinach
225g/8oz ricotta cheese, crumbled
90g/3oz Parmesan cheese, finely grated
Salt and freshly ground pepper
Pinch freshly grated nutmeg
1 egg, lightly beaten
45g/3 tbsps butter

1. Defrost the spinach and press it between two plates to extract all the moisture.

Step 1 Press the spinach between two plates to remove excess moisture

2. Mix the spinach with the ricotta cheese, half the Parmesan cheese, the salt, pepper and nutmeg. Gradually add the egg, beating well until the mixture holds together when shaped.

3. With floured hands, shape the mixture into oval shapes. Use about 15ml/1 tbsp mixture for each gnocchi.

4. Lower into simmering water 3 or 4 at a time and allow to cook gently until the gnocchi float to the surface (about 1-2 minutes).

5. Remove with a draining spoon and place in a well buttered ovenproof dish.

6. When all the gnocchi are cooked, sprinkle on the re-

Step 3 Shape the gnocchi mixture with well-floured hands into ovals or balls.

Step 4 The gnocchi will float to the surface of the water when cooked. Remove with a draining spoon.

maining Parmesan cheese and dot with the remaining butter.

7. Reheat for 10 minutes in a hot oven and brown under a preheated grill before serving.

Cook's Notes

Time
Preparation takes 15 minutes, cooking takes about 20 minutes.

Variation
Accompany with a tomato or cheese sauce and a salad for a light meal.

Vitamin Content
Spinach is a good source of vitamin A and the cheese provides vitamin B.

SERVES 4

COURGETTE SALAD

Raw vegetables are full of vitamins, and courgette in particular has a delicious taste and texture.

225g/8oz macaroni
4 tomatoes
4-5 courgettes, sliced thinly
8 stuffed green olives, sliced
90ml/6 tbsps French dressing

1. Put the macaroni into a large saucepan and cover with boiling water. Add a little salt and simmer for 10 minutes, or until tender but still firm. Rinse in cold water and drain well.

2. Cut a small cross in the tops of each tomato and plunge into boiling water for 30 seconds.

3. Carefully remove the skins from the blanched tomatoes, using a sharp knife. Chop the tomatoes coarsely.

4. Mix all the ingredients in a large bowl and chill in the refrigerator for 30 minutes before serving.

Step 1 Rinse the macaroni in lots of cold water, then drain well forking it occasionally to prevent it sticking together.

Step 4 Mix all the ingredients together well, stirring thoroughly to blend the dressing in evenly.

Cook's Notes

Time
Preparation takes 15 minutes, cooking takes approximately 10 minutes.

Variation
Use any other pasta shape of your choice.

Preparation
If you prefer, the courgettes can be blanched in boiling water for 1 minute, then drained and cooled before mixing with the salad ingredients.

Vitamin Content
This recipe is high in vitamin C from the courgettes and tomatoes, vitamin A from the tomatoes and vitamin B from the pasta.

SERVES 4-6

WATERCRESS AND ORANGE SALAD

This colourful salad combination is ideal served with cold meats or fish.

3 large bunches of watercress
4 oranges
90ml/6 tbsps vegetable oil
Juice and rind of 1 orange
Pinch sugar
5ml/1 tsp lemon juice
Salt and freshly ground black pepper

1. Wash the watercress and carefully cut away any thick stalks. Break the watercress into small sprigs, discarding any yellow leaves.
2. Carefully remove the peel and pith from the oranges using a sharp knife. Catch any juice that spills in a small bowl.
3. Cutting carefully, remove the fleshy segments from between the thin membrane inside the orange. Squeeze any juice from the orange membrane into the bowl with the juice from the peel.

Step 1 Break the watercress into small sprigs, discarding any yellow leaves as you go.

4. Arrange the watercress with the orange segments on a serving dish.

5. Put the remaining ingredients into the bowl with the reserved orange juice, and mix together well.

6. Pour the salad dressing over the oranges and watercress just before serving, to prevent the watercress from going limp.

Step 2 Carefully peel the oranges using a sharp knife, and collecting any juices in a small bowl.

Step 3 Cut the orange segments carefully from between the inner membranes using a sharp knife.

Cook's Notes

Time
Preparation takes approximately 20 minutes.

Serving Idea
Serve this salad on a bed of finely grated carrot.

Variation
Use grapefruit instead of the oranges, and chicory instead of the watercress.

Vitamin Content
This salad is extremely high in vitamin C, and if served with carrot is also a good source of vitamin A.

SERVES 4

CHEESE SALAD

This cheese salad is distinctly Greek in origin, and is ideal as a starter as well as being substantial enough to serve as a light lunch.

½ small head of endive or Crisp lettuce
½ small Iceberg lettuce
1 small cucumber
4 large tomatoes
8-10 pitted green or black olives, halved
1 medium-sized Spanish or red onion, peeled and sliced
125g/4oz feta cheese
75ml/5 tbsps olive oil
30ml/2 tbsps red wine vinegar
5ml/1 tsp chopped fresh oregano
2.5ml/½ tsp freshly ground sea salt
1.25ml/¼ tsp freshly ground black pepper
2.5ml/½ tsp ready made German mustard

1. Wash the endive and lettuce leaves thoroughly. Pat them dry with kitchen paper and tear into bite-sized pieces.

2. Thinly slice the cucumber, peeling it if you wish.

3. Cut a small cross into the top of each tomato and plunge into boiling water for 30 seconds.

4. Carefully peel the skins from the blanched tomatoes and slice the flesh crosswise.

5. Put the endive, lettuce, cucumber, tomatoes, olives and onion into a serving bowl and toss them together until well mixed.

6. Cut the feta cheese into 1cm/½-inch cubes. Sprinkle

Step 1 Tear the lettuce and endive into pieces to prevent excessive bruising and destruction of vitamins in the leaves.

Step 4 Using a sharp knife, slice the peeled tomatoes crosswise.

these cubes over the salad in the serving bowl.

7. Put all the remaining ingredients into a small bowl and whisk together using a fork or small whisk.

8. Pour the dressing over the salad and serve immediately.

Cook's Notes

 Time
Preparation takes 10-12 minutes.

 Serving Idea
Serve with jacket potatoes or crusty French bread.

 Variation
Use Cheddar or Cheshire cheese in place of the feta cheese.

 Vitamin Content
Leaf vegetables such as lettuce are an excellent source of vitamin K. The tomatoes and cucumber are high in vitamin C and the cheese is a good source of vitamins B and D.

SERVES 6

ROGNONS À LA DIJONNAISE

This delicious French dish makes good use of vitamin-rich kidneys, an offal which is often very underused in cookery.

750g/1½lbs lambs' kidneys
60g/2oz unsalted butter
1-2 shallots, finely chopped
280ml/½ pint dry white wine
90g/3oz lightly salted butter, softened
45ml/3 tbsps Dijon mustard
Salt, black pepper and lemon juice, to taste
30ml/2 tbsps chopped parsley

Step 2 Trim away any hard core from the centre of each kidney half using a small pair of sharp scissors.

Step 1 Trim the fat from each kidney and cut them in half lengthways.

Step 8 Whisk the butter, mustard, salt, pepper and lemon juice into the reduced sauce using a fork or small whisk and beating until it is thick.

1. Trim away any fat from the kidneys and slice them in half lengthways.

2. Carefully snip out any hard core from the centre using a pair of sharp scissors.

3. Melt the unsalted butter in a large frying pan and gently sauté the kidneys, uncovered, until they are light brown on all sides.

4. Remove the kidneys from the frying pan and keep them warm.

5. Add the shallots to the meat juices in the pan and cook

for about 1 minute, stirring frequently until they are just soft.

6. Add the wine and bring to the boil, stirring constantly and scraping the pan to remove any browned juices.

7. Boil this sauce rapidly for 3-4 minutes to reduce by about half. Remove the pan from the heat.

8. Put the softened butter into the pan with the mustard and seasonings. Whisk the mixture into the reduced sauce with a small whisk or fork.

9. Return the pan to the heat and add the kidneys and the parsley. Heat very gently for 1-2 minutes, taking care not to boil the mixture any further. Serve immediately.

Cook's Notes

Time
Preparation takes approximately 25 minutes, cooking takes 15-17 minutes.

Watchpoint
Do not overcook the kidneys or they will become tough.

Vitamin Content
Kidneys are an excellent source of vitamins A, B and D.

SERVES 6

PORK PROVENÇALE

This hearty casserole of lean pork topped with potatoes is suitable for serving as a family meal, or as part of a dinner party menu.

1 kg/2lbs pork fillets
60g/2oz butter
350g/12oz onions, peeled and thinly sliced
425g/15oz tin tomatoes
Salt and freshly ground black pepper
1.25ml/¼ tsp dried mixed herbs
750g/1½lbs potatoes, peeled and thinly sliced
15ml/1 tbsp chopped parsley for garnish

1. Trim the pork of any surplus fat and slice into thin strips.

2. Melt half of the butter in a large sauté pan and gently fry

the slices of meat, stirring continuously to prevent them from burning.

3. Transfer the meat to a plate and set aside.

4. Stir the onions into the meat juices in the sauté pan and cook gently until just soft.

5. Add the tomatoes to the pan along with the salt, pepper and mixed herbs. Bring to the boil, then simmer gently for about 5 minutes, or until the sauce has reduced by about a third.

6. Arrange the meat, sauce and potatoes in layers in an ovenproof serving dish, finishing with a layer of potato.

7. Melt the remaining butter and brush the top layer of potato with this.

8. Cover the dish with a lid or foil, and cook in the oven for 1½ hours at 180°C/350°F/Gas Mark 4.

9. Remove the lid from the dish and continue cooking for a further 30 minutes to brown the potatoes. Sprinkle with chopped parsley before serving.

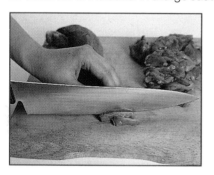

Step 1 Slice the pork into thin strips using a sharp knife.

Step 4 Gently fry the onions in the meat juices until they are just soft.

Step 6 Arrange the meat, tomato sauce and potatoes in layers in an ovenproof serving dish.

Cook's Notes

Time
Preparation takes 25 minutes, cooking takes approximately 2 hours.

Freezing
This dish will freeze very well for up to 3 months. Freeze it before the final 30 minutes cooking time, then reheat by thawing and cooking uncovered for 1 hour at 180°C/350°F/Gas Mark 4.

Vitamin Content
The vegetables are a good source of vitamin C, and the tomatoes also contain vitamin A.

SERVES 4
LENTIL KEDGEREE

This delicious recipe combines spiced rice with lentils and onion to make a substantial vegetarian lunch or supper dish.

225g/8oz basmati rice
225g/8oz red lentils
750ml/1¼ pints warm water
120g/4oz butter, or olive oil
1 medium-sized onion, peeled and chopped
2.5ml/½ tsp crushed fresh root ginger
2.5ml/½ tsp crushed garlic
2.5cm/1-inch piece cinnamon stick
6 cloves
1 bay leaf
5ml/1 tsp ground coriander
1.25ml/¼ tsp ground turmeric
2.5ml/½ tsp freshly ground sea salt
2 green chillies, sliced in half lengthways

1. Wash the rice and the lentils thoroughly in cold water. Drain well.

2. Put the drained rice and lentils into a large bowl and cover with the warm water. Soak for 30 minutes, then drain very thoroughly, reserving the water.

3. Heat the butter or olive oil in a large saucepan. Stir in the onion and fry gently for 2-3 minutes, stirring to prevent from burning.

4. Add the ginger, garlic, cinnamon stick, cloves and bay leaf to the onion and continue frying for 1 minute.

5. Add the rice and lentils to the fried onion, along with the coriander, turmeric, salt and green chilli. Stir over the heat for 2-3 minutes, until the rice and lentils are evenly coated

Step 5 Stir-fry the rice and lentils together, making sure that they are evenly coated with the fat.

Step 6 Cook the rice and lentils until all the liquid has been absorbed, then fluff up with a fork before serving.

with fat.

6. Pour the reserved water into the rice mixture and bring to the boil. Reduce the heat and cover the pan with a tight fitting lid. Simmer for 8-10 minutes without stirring, or until the water has been completely absorbed.

7. Stir the rice and lentils together, remove and discard the chillies, and serve immediately.

Cook's Notes

Time
Preparation takes 15 minutes, plus soaking time. Cooking takes approximately 30 minutes.

 Watchpoint
Great care must be taken when using fresh chillies. If any of the juice gets into your mouth or eyes, rinse with lots of cold water.

Vitamin Content
Lentils and rice are both excellent sources of vitamin B.

SERVES 4

LENTIL AND VEGETABLE CURRY

Lentils are a staple ingredient in Indian cookery. This delicious vegetable curry should be made using fresh spices for the best flavour.

225g/8oz whole green lentils
30ml/2 tbsps vegetable oil
5ml/1 tsp salt
2.5ml/½ tsp mustard seed, crushed
5ml/1 tsp ground coriander
2.5ml/½ tsp ground cumin
2 dried red chillies, crushed
1 carrot, peeled and sliced diagonally
1 potato, peeled and cubed
6-8 okra, topped and tailed, then cut into 2.5cm/1-inch
   pieces
1 small courgette, sliced diagonally
1 small aubergine, halved and sliced
375ml/¾ pint water
6 curry leaves
1 green chilli, slit.in half and chopped
5ml/1 tsp fresh chopped mint
15ml/1 tbsp fresh chopped coriander
Coriander leaves for garnish

1. Wash the lentils in warm water until it runs clear. Drain well.

2. Put the lentils into a large saucepan and pour over 570ml/1 pint water. Simmer gently for 15-20 minutes.

3. When the lentils are soft, beat with a potato masher or whisk until they are puréed.

4. In a large saucepan heat the oil and gently fry the mustard seed, ground coriander, cumin and dried chillies for 1 minute.

5. Add the vegetables to the spices and cook for 2 minutes, stirring all the time, to coat them evenly in the oil and spice mixture.

6. Add the water and the puréed lentils to the vegetable mixture and stir well.

7. Add the curry leaves, chopped chilli, mint and fresh coriander, then cook for 15 minutes. Serve hot, garnished with coriander leaves.

Step 3 Using a potato masher or whisk, break up the cooked lentils until they are well puréed.

Step 6 Stir the puréed lentils into the vegetable mixture.

Cook's Notes

Time
Preparation takes about 10 minutes, cooking takes 20-30 minutes.

Variation
Use any combination of fresh vegetables to vary this curry.

Serving Idea
Serve with boiled basmati rice.

Vitamin Content
Lentils provide an excellent source of vitamin B and fresh vegetables provide vitamins A and C.

SERVES 4

BEEF WITH PINEAPPLE AND PEPPERS

This delicious sweet and sour main course is distinctly Chinese in origin.

450g/1lb fillet or rump steak
1 small pineapple
1 green pepper
1 red pepper
15ml/1 tbsp peanut oil
1 onion, peeled and roughly chopped
2 cloves garlic, crushed
2.5cm/1-inch fresh root ginger, peeled and thinly sliced
5ml/1 tsp sesame oil
30ml/2 tbsps light soy sauce
15ml/1 tbsp dark soy sauce
5ml/1 tsp sugar
15ml/1 tbsp brown sauce
60ml/4 tbsps water
Salt and freshly ground black pepper

1. Using a sharp knife, cut the steak into thin strips.

2. Carefully peel the pineapple and cut out any eyes using a sharp knife or potato peeler. Cut the pineapple into slices and chop them into bite-sized pieces, removing the hard core.

3. Slice the green and red peppers in half. Remove and discard the cores and seeds. Chop the pepper flesh into thin strips.

4. Heat the peanut oil in a wok or large frying pan, and gently fry the onion, garlic and ginger, stirring continuously until the onion has softened slightly.

5. Add the strips of beef and the strips of pepper, and continue stir-frying for 3 minutes.

6. Add the pineapple and stir-fry again for 2 minutes.

7. Remove the meat, vegetables and fruit from the wok, and put on a plate. Set aside.

8. Stir the sesame oil into the juices in the wok and add the soy sauces, sugar, brown sauce and water. Simmer rapidly for 30 seconds to reduce and thicken.

9. Stir the fruit, vegetables and beef back into the sauce. Season, heat through and serve immediately.

Step 1 Using a sharp knife, cut the steak into thin strips.

Step 5 Stir-fry the beef and peppers with the onions in the wok.

Cook's Notes

Time
Preparation takes 30 minutes, cooking takes about 10 minutes.

Serving Idea
Serve with spring rolls and plain boiled rice.

Watchpoint
Take care not to overcook the meat and vegetables, as this will greatly reduce the vitamin content of this dish.

V Vitamin Content
Steak is an excellent source of vitamin B and the vegetables and fruit are high in vitamin C.

SERVES 4
KIDNEYS WITH BACON

Stir-frying is an excellent way of cooking kidneys, as the speedy cooking ensures that they do not become tough.

450g/1lb lambs' kidneys
30ml/2 tbsps vegetable oil
8 rashers lean bacon, cut into 2.5cm/1-inch strips
1 onion, peeled and chopped
3 cloves garlic, crushed
15ml/1 tbsp tomato chutney
15ml/1 tbsp light soy sauce
30ml/2 tbsps water
Salt and freshly ground black pepper
15ml/1 tbsp cornflour
45ml/3 tbsps sherry
22ml/1½ tbsps fresh chopped parsley

1. Trim the fat from the kidneys and cut each kidney in half with a sharp knife.

2. Carefully trim out the hard core from the centre of each kidney with a sharp knife or scissors.

3. Cut a lattice design on the back of each kidney using a sharp knife and taking care not to cut right through.

4. Put the kidneys into a bowl and stir in the sherry. Set aside for 15 minutes to marinate.

5. Heat the oil in a large wok and fry the bacon, onion and garlic for 5 minutes, stirring continuously to prevent burning. Remove from the wok and set aside on a plate.

6. Drain the kidneys and reserve the sherry marinade. Add the kidneys to the wok and stir for 3 minutes only.

7. Stir the tomato chutney, soy sauce and water into the wok with the kidneys, then add the bacon and onion mixture. Season with salt and pepper and stir-fry gently for 5 minutes.

8. Blend the cornflour with the sherry marinade.

9. Add 1 tbsp parsley to the cornflour mixture and stir this

Step 2 Remove the hard core from each kidney half using a sharp knife or a small pair of scissors.

Step 3 Cut a lattice design on the backs of each kidney, using a sharp knife, and taking care not to cut right through.

Step 6 Stir-fry the kidneys until they are completely browned.

into the kidneys in the wok, mixing well until the sauce is thickened and smooth. Serve at once, sprinkled with a little extra parsley.

Cook's Notes

Time
Preparation takes 20 minutes, cooking takes 25 minutes.

Serving Idea
Serve with rice or creamed potatoes.

Vitamin Content
All offal is an excellent source of vitamins A, B and D.

SERVES 4
MONKFISH AND PEPPER KEBABS

Monkfish is ideal for making kebabs as it can be cut into firm cubes which do not disintegrate during cooking.

8 rashers of lean bacon, rind removed
450g/1lb monkfish, skinned and cut into 2.5cm/1-inch pieces
1 small green pepper, seeded and cut into 2.5cm/1-inch pieces
1 small red pepper, seeded and cut into 2.5cm/1-inch pieces
12 small mushroom caps
8 bay leaves
45ml/3 tbsps vegetable oil
120ml/4 fl oz dry white wine
60ml/4 tbsps tarragon vinegar
2 shallots, finely chopped
15ml/1 tbsp chopped fresh tarragon
15ml/1 tbsp chopped fresh chervil or parsley
225g/8oz butter, softened
Salt and freshly ground black pepper

Step 2 Wrap each piece of fish in one of the strips of bacon.

Step 8 Add the butter gradually into the simmering wine, whisking briskly to thicken the sauce.

1. Cut the bacon rashers in half lengthways and then again in half crosswise.

2. Put a piece of the fish onto each piece of bacon and roll the bacon around the piece of fish.

3. Thread the bacon and fish rolls onto large skewers, alternating them with slices of pepper, mushroom and the bay leaves.

4. Brush the kebabs with oil and arrange on a grill pan.

5. Preheat the grill to hot and cook the kebabs for 10-15 minutes, turning them frequently to prevent the kebabs from burning.

6. Heat the white wine, vinegar and shallots in a small saucepan until boiling. Cook rapidly to reduce by half.

7. Add the herbs and lower the heat.

8. Using a fork or small whisk beat the butter bit by bit into the hot wine mixture, whisking rapidly until the sauce becomes thick. Season to taste.

9. Arrange the kebabs on a serving plate and serve with a little of the sauce spooned over and the remainder in a separate jug.

Cook's Notes

Time
Preparation takes 30 minutes, cooking will take about 25 minutes.

Preparation
When making the sauce it is important to whisk briskly, or it will not thicken sufficiently.

Vitamin Content
Fish is an excellent source of vitamins A and D. Bacon is a good source of vitamin B, and peppers are high in vitamin C.

SERVES 4

SWORDFISH STEAKS WITH GREEN PEPPERCORNS AND GARLIC SAUCE

Swordfish steaks are delicious and are now easily available at most good fishmongers.

30ml/2 tbsps fresh green peppercorns
90ml/6 tbsps lemon juice
60ml/4 tbsps olive oil
Freshly ground sea salt
4 swordfish steaks
1 egg
1 clove garlic, roughly chopped
140ml/¼ pint oil
30ml/2 tsps fresh oregano
Salt and freshly ground black pepper

1. Crush the green peppercorns lightly using a pestle and mortar.

2. Mix the lemon juice, olive oil and salt into the lightly crushed green peppercorns.

3. Place the swordfish steaks in a shallow ovenproof dish and pour the lemon and oil mixture over each steak. Re-frigerate overnight, turning occasionally until the fish becomes opaque.

4. Using a blender or food processor, mix together the eggs and garlic.

5. With the machine still running, gradually pour the oil through the funnel in a thin steady stream onto the egg and garlic mixture. Continue to blend until the sauce is thick.

6. Remove the leaves from the oregano sprigs and chop them finely.

7. Preheat the grill to hot and arrange the swordfish on the grill pan.

8. Sprinkle the chopped oregano over the swordfish steaks and season well. Cook for 15 minutes, turning them frequently and basting with the lemon and pepper marinade.

9. When the steaks are cooked, place onto a serving dish and spoon the garlic mayonnaise over to serve.

Step 1 Lightly crush the green peppercorns using a pestle and mortar.

Step 3 Marinate the swordfish steaks overnight, after such time they should be opaque.

Cook's Notes

Time
Preparation takes 25 minutes, plus overnight soaking.
Cooking takes about 15 minutes.

Variation
Substitute 30ml/2 tbsps well rinsed canned green peppercorns in place of the fresh peppercorns if you cannot get these, and use tuna steaks instead of the swordfish if you prefer.

Serving Idea
Serve with jacket potatoes and fresh salad.

Vitamin Content
The fish contains vitamins B and D.

SERVES 4
TARRAGON GRILLED RED MULLET

Red mullet is a very decorative little fish that is now readily available at fishmongers and supermarkets.

4 large or 8 small red mullets, gutted, scaled, washed and dried
4 or 8 sprigs of fresh tarragon
60ml/4 tbsps vegetable oil
30ml/2 tbsps tarragon vinegar
Salt and freshly ground black pepper
1 egg
5ml/1 tsp Dijon mustard
120ml/4 fl oz sunflower oil
15ml/1 tbsp wine vinegar
5ml/1 tsp brandy
15ml/1 tbsp chopped fresh tarragon
15ml/1 tbsp chopped fresh parsley
15ml/1 tbsp double cream

1. Rub the inside of each mullet with a teaspoonful of salt, scrubbing hard to remove any discoloured membranes inside. Rinse thoroughly.

2. Place a sprig of fresh tarragon inside each fish.

3. Using a sharp knife cut 2 diagonal slits on the side of each fish.

4. Mix together the vegetable oil, tarragon vinegar and a little salt and pepper in a small bowl.

5. Arrange the fish on a shallow dish and pour over the tarragon, vinegar marinade, brushing some of the mixture into the cuts on the side of the fish. Refrigerate for 30 minutes.

6. Put the egg into a blender or food processor along with the mustard and a little salt and pepper. Process for 2-3 seconds to mix.

7. With the machine running, add the oil through the funnel in a thin steady stream. Continue blending the dressing until it is thick and creamy.

8. Add the vinegar, brandy and herbs, and process for a further 30 seconds to mix well.

9. Lightly whip the cream with a small whisk until it thickens.

10. Fold the slightly thickened cream carefully into the oil and vinegar dressing. Pour into a serving dish and refrigerate until ready to use.

11. Arrange the fish on a grill pan and cook under a preheated hot grill for 5-8 minutes per side, depending on the size of the fish. Baste frequently with the marinade while cooking, then serve with a little of the sauce and some sprigs of fresh tarragon, if you like.

Step 1 Rub the insides of each fish with a teaspoonful of salt, scrubbing briskly to remove any discoloured membranes.

Step 3 Using a sharp knife, cut 2 diagonal slits on the side of each fish, taking great care not to cut right through the flesh.

Cook's Notes

Time
Preparation takes about 15 minutes, cooking takes 10-16 minutes.

Variation
Use herrings or mackerel in place of the mullet.

Vitamin Content
All fish is an excellent source of vitamins A and D.

DUCK WITH ORANGES

This traditional combination is given extra flavour by cooking the duck in a distinctly oriental manner.

3 oranges
1 duck
15g/½oz butter
15ml/1 tbsp oil
280ml/½ pint light chicken stock
90ml/3 fl oz red wine
30ml/2 tbsps redcurrant jelly
Salt and freshly ground black pepper
5ml/1 tsp arrowroot
15ml/1 tbsp cold water

1. Using a potato peeler carefully pare the rind thinly off 2 of the oranges.

Step 2 Using a sharp knife carefully cut the parred orange rind into very thin strips.

2. Cut the rind into very fine shreds using a sharp knife. Put the shredded orange rind into a small bowl and cover with boiling water. Set aside to blanch for 5 minutes, then drain.

3. Squeeze the juice from the 2 oranges. Set this aside.

4. Cut away the peel and the pith from the remaining orange and then slice the flesh into thin rounds. Set aside.

5. Wash the duck and dry well with absorbent kitchen paper.

6. Put the butter and the oil into a large wok and heat until melted. Add the duck and fry, turning frequently until it is brown all over.

7. Remove the duck from the wok, cool slightly and using poultry shears, cut away the leg and wing ends. Cut the duck in half lengthways and then cut each half into 2.5cm/1-inch strips.

8. Remove the fat from the wok and return the duck to the wok. Add the stock, red wine, redcurrant jelly, squeezed orange juice, and the well drained strips of rind. Bring to the boil, then season to taste. Reduce the heat, cover the

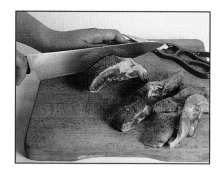

Step 7 Cut each half of the duck into 2.5cm/1-inch strips using poultry shears or a very sharp knife.

wok and simmer the duck gently for 20 minutes, or until well cooked.

9. Skim away any surface fat and thicken the sauce by mixing the arrowroot with the water and stirring into the wok. Bring the mixture back to the boil and simmer for a further 5 minutes, or until the sauce is thick.

10. Arrange the duck on a serving plate and garnish with the orange slices and some additional watercress if liked.

Cook's Notes

Time
Preparation takes 30 minutes, cooking takes 35 minutes.

Serving Idea
Serve with plain boiled rice or sautéed potatoes.

Vitamin Content
Duck is a good source of vitamin B, and oranges are an excellent source of vitamin C.

LIVER WITH ONIONS

This dish is simple to prepare, but absolutely delicious and highly nutritious.

450g/1lb onions
450g/1lb lambs' liver, thinly sliced
Salt and freshly ground black pepper
45g/1½oz plain flour
45ml/3 tbsps vegetable oil
30g/1 oz butter
30ml/2 tbsps fresh chopped parsley

1. Peel the onions and slice thinly, keeping each slice in

Step 1 Using a sharp knife, thinly slice the peeled onions, keeping them in rings if possible.

circles if possible.

2. Trim away any large pipes or tubes from the liver using a pair of small scissors or a sharp knife.

3. Mix the seasoning and the flour together on a plate and lay the slices of liver into the flour, turning them and pressing them gently to coat all over evenly.

4. Put the oil and the butter into a large frying pan. Heat

Step 2 Trim away any pipes or tubes from the liver slices using a small pair of scissors or a sharp knife

Step 3 Coat each liver slice thoroughly with the seasoned flour, pressing it gently onto the surface.

gently until foaming.

5. Add the onion rings and fry until just golden.

6. Add the liver slices and fry for 3-5 minutes on each side until well cooked. Cooking time will depend on the thickness of each slice.

7. Stir the parsley into the liver and onions and serve immediately on hot plates.

Cook's Notes

Time
Preparation takes 15 minutes, cooking takes about 10 minutes.

Variation
Add 120g/4oz shredded streaky bacon with the onions.

Serving Idea
Serve with creamed potatoes and green vegetables.

Watchpoint
Do not overcook liver or any offal, as it will toughen.

Freezing
Liver freezes well, but should be frozen before cooking.

Vitamin Content
Onions are a good source of vitamin C. Liver is an excellent source of vitamins A, B and D.

SERVES 4

'BURNT' CREAM

The gentle cooking of this creamy dessert ensures that the valuable vitamin content in the cream is not decreased in any way.

280ml/½ pint full cream milk
280ml/½ pint double cream
5 egg yolks
60g/2oz caster sugar
Few drops of vanilla essence
90g/3oz soft brown sugar
140ml/¼ pint whipped double cream (optional)

1. Put the milk and the cream into a heavy-based saucepan and heat gently until almost boiling. Remove from the heat and set aside to cool slightly.

2. Put the egg yolks, sugar and vanilla into a bowl and whisk vigorously until they become light and creamy.

3. Strain the milk and cream through a sieve into a large jug.

4. Gradually add the strained milk and cream onto the egg yolk mixture, beating vigorously and constantly as you pour.

5. Rinse the saucepan clean and dry it. Return the egg yolk and cream mixture to the saucepan and heat gently, stirring constantly with a wooden spoon, until the mixture becomes a thick and creamy custard.

6. Do not allow the custard to boil or it will curdle.

7. Strain the custard through a sieve into a shallow serving dish. The custard should come almost to the top of the dish.

8. Stand the custard in a refrigerator and chill until set, preferably overnight.

9. Sprinkle the brown sugar thickly over the surface of the set custard.

10. Stand the custard under a preheated hot grill and cook until the sugar melts and caramelises. Remove the 'burnt cream' from the grill and chill it until the sugar layer is a hard, crisp caramel.

11. Serve very cold, decorated with piped double cream if desired.

Step 2 Whisk the egg yolk, sugar and vanilla together until thick and creamy. The mixture is ready when you can leave a trail on the surface as it is lifted with a spoon or whisk.

Step 10 Grill the brown sugar on the top of the chilled custard until it melts and caramelises.

Cook's Notes

Time
Preparation takes about 15 minutes, cooking takes about 30 minutes, plus chilling time.

Preparation
The custard is ready when the mixture coats the back of a wooden spoon.

Watchpoint
Take great care never to boil the mixture at any stage, or it will curdle. If this should happen, blend 30g/1oz cornflour with a little milk and stir this into the hot curdled mixture, continue stirring until it thickens and becomes smooth.

Serving Idea
Serve with crisp biscuits or a fresh fruit salad.

Vitamin Content
Cream and milk contain vitamins A, B and D. Never expose cream or milk to sunlight, as this will destroy the valuable vitamin B.

SERVES 4

RICE PUDDING

Rice pudding has always been a firm family favourite and this recipe adds spices to make it special enough even for dinner parties.

60g/2oz unsalted butter
1 bay leaf, crumbled
2.5cm/1-inch piece cinnamon stick, crushed
175g/6oz pudding rice, washed and drained
1.2 ltrs/2 pints milk
400ml/⅔ pint evaporated milk
175g/6oz granulated sugar
60g/2oz chopped blanched almonds
Seeds of 8 small cardamoms, crushed
30g/1oz pistachio nuts, chopped or cut into slivers

1. Melt the butter in a saucepan and fry the bay leaf and cinnamon for 1 minute.

2. Add the rice and stir well to coat evenly with the melted fat.

3. Add the milk and bring the mixture to the boil, then reduce the heat and simmer for 40-50 minutes, stirring occasionally to prevent the rice from sticking to the pan.

4. Add the sugar and the evaporated milk to the rice mixture and continue cooking for a further 20-30 minutes, stirring frequently to prevent burning.

5. It is important to keep stirring the mixture during this cooking time to bring up thin layers of light brown skin which form on the base of the saucepan. This is what gives the pudding its rich, reddish tinge and caramel flavour.

6. Add the chopped almonds and the crushed cardamom seeds to the rice puddings. Stir well and pour into a large serving dish.

7. Decorate the top of the rice pudding with the slivered pistachio nuts, and serve hot or cold.

Step 2 Stir the rice into the fried bay leaf and cinnamon, mixing well to coat each grain evenly with the flavoured fat.

Step 5 Stir the pudding frequently to bring up the thin layers of light brown skin which will form on the base of the saucepan during cooking.

Step 7 Decorate the pudding with slivered pistachios before serving.

Cook's Notes

 Time
Preparation takes 10 minutes, cooking takes 1 hour 30 minutes.

 Watchpoint
Frequent stirring is important in this recipe to prevent the sugar from caramelising too much and giving a bitter flavour to the dessert.

Vitamin Content
Rice contains vitamins from the B group, and milk and evaporated milk contain vitamins A and D.

SERVES 4-6
SUMMER PUDDING

This favourite summer dessert simply oozes vitamins and flavour.

750g/1½lbs fresh soft fruit, e.g. raspberries, strawberries, rhubarb, redcurrants, blackcurrants or any combination of these fruits
175g/6oz granulated sugar
10 thick slices of white bread, crusts removed
420ml/¾ pint fresh cream
450g/1lb fresh whole raspberries

1. Put the 1½lbs of mixed fruit into a large saucepan and stir in the sugar.

2. Heat the fruit gently, shaking the pan vigorously so that the sugar dissolves but the fruit stays as intact as possible. Remove from the heat and cool completely.

3. Cut the slices of bread into thick fingers and use them to line the base and sides of a 900 ml/1½ pint pudding basin. Press the slices of bread together as firmly as possible to avoid leaving any gaps between them.

4. Pour the cooled fruit and the juice into the centre of the pudding, and cover the top completely with the remaining bread. Press down firmly.

5. Place a saucer or small plate over the top of the pudding and weigh this down with cans of food or balance scale weights.

6. Chill the pudding overnight in the refrigerator.

7. Remove the weights and the small plate or saucer. Loosen the sides of the pudding carefully with a round bladed knife, and invert a serving plate over the top of the bowl.

8. Carefully turn both the serving plate and the bowl over, and shake gently. The pudding should drop onto the serving plate.

9. Whip the cream until it is thick, then spread approximately half of the cream over the summer pudding.

Step 2 Shake the fruit and sugar together gently over a low heat until the sugar dissolves, but the fruit remains mainly intact.

Step 3 Press the slices of bread together well around the sides and the base of the pudding dish, trying to make sure that there are no gaps in between each slice.

Step 10 Press the whole raspberries into the cream layer covering the summer pudding.

10. Press the fresh raspberries onto the cream in a thick layer all over the pudding, and pipe the remaining cream in small rosettes between the gaps.

11. Chill well, before serving.

Cook's Notes

 Time
Preparation takes approximately 30 minutes, plus overnight chilling.

Freezing
This pudding freezes extremely well, but should be decorated with the fruit and cream after it has been thawed.

Vitamin Content
The bread contains vitamin B, the fruit contains vitamin C, and the cream contains vitamin D.

SERVES 4-6

CARROTELLA

Carrots have a natural sweetness which lends itself to sweet as well as savoury dishes. Carrotella is a sweet and spicy dessert which should be served very cold.

1.2 lts/2 pints milk
450g/1lb carrots, peeled and finely grated
190ml/⅓ pint evaporated milk
120g/4oz granulated sugar
60g/2oz sultanas
Seeds of 8 small cardamoms, crushed
2 drops vanilla essence
30g/1oz chopped blanched almonds
30g/1oz chopped pistachio nuts

1. Put the milk into a saucepan and simmer over a low heat until reduced to about 850ml/1½ pints.

2. Add the carrots. Cover and cook over a medium heat for approximately 15 minutes, or until the carrots have begun to soften.

3. Stir in the evaporated milk, sugar and sultanas, re-cover and simmer gently for about another 5 minutes.

4. Remove the saucepan from the heat, then stir in the crushed cardamom seed and vanilla essence.

5. Beat the carrotella briskly to break up the carrots, then turn into a serving dish and cool slightly.

6. Sprinkle the nuts on top and chill very well before serving.

Step 2 Cook the carrots over a medium heat for 15 minutes, or until they have softened and are breaking up.

Step 6 Sprinkle the partially chilled carrotella with the chopped and flaked nuts.

Cook's Notes

Time
Preparation takes 15 minutes. Cooking takes 40 minutes, plus chilling time.

Serving Idea
Serve with a spoonful of chilled fromage frais.

Variation
Use rosewater instead of the vanilla essence, and finely chopped hazelnuts instead of the pistachio nuts.

V Vitamin Content
Milk and evaporated milk contain vitamins D and E. Carrots are an excellent source of vitamins A and C.

SERVES 4

BROWN BREAD ICE CREAM

This unusual ice cream is easy to make and is an ideal standby dessert to keep in the freezer.

2 egg yolks
60g/2oz caster sugar
450ml/¾ pint double, or whipping cream
Few drops of vanilla essence
240ml/8 fl oz water
180g/6oz soft brown sugar
90ml/6 tbsps fresh brown breadcrumbs
5ml/1 tsp ground cinnamon

1. Put the egg yolks and the caster sugar into a bowl, and whisk vigorously with an electric beater until thick, pale and creamy.

2. Pour in the double cream and continue whisking until thick and creamy.

3. Beat in the vanilla essence, then pour the cream mixture into a freezer-proof container and freeze for 1 hour, or until beginning to set around the edges.

4. Break the ice cream away from the edges and whisk with the electric beater until the ice crystals have broken. Return to the freezer and chill for a further hour. Repeat this procedure 2 more times, then freeze completely.

5. Put the water and the brown sugar into a small saucepan and heat gently, stirring until the sugar has dissolved. Bring the mixture to the boil and boil rapidly until the sugar caramelises.

6. Remove the caramel sugar from the heat and stir in the breadcrumbs and the cinnamon.

7. Spread the caramel mixture onto a baking sheet lined with oiled greaseproof paper, and allow to set.

8. Break up the caramelised breadcrumbs by placing

Step 1 Whisk the eggs and caster sugar together until they are pale, thick and creamy.

Step 7 When cooled, the caramelised breadcrumbs should set completely hard.

them in plastic food bags and crushing with a rolling pin.

9. Turn the frozen ice cream into a large bowl and break it up with a fork.

10. Allow the ice cream to soften slightly, then stir in the caramelised breadcrumbs, mixing thoroughly to blend evenly.

11. Return the brown bread ice cream to the freezer tray and freeze completely.

12. Allow the mixture to soften for 10 minutes before serving in scoops with a crisp biscuit.

Cook's Notes

Time
Preparation takes approximately 40 minutes, plus freezing time.

Preparation
Be very careful when making the caramel sugar as it can burn very easily.

Vitamin Content
Wholemeal bread contains vitamins B and E. Fresh cream contains vitamins A, B and D.

SERVES 4-6

FRUITY BREAD PUDDING

This traditional family pudding is made extra nutritious by using wholemeal bread and a rich assortment of dried fruits.

120g/4oz raisins
120g/4oz currants
120g/4oz sultanas
120g/4oz prunes, stoned and chopped
Finely grated rind and juice of 1 orange
8 thick slices wholemeal bread, crusts removed
60g/2oz butter, softened
120g/4oz soft brown sugar
280ml/½ pint whole milk
2 eggs, lightly beaten
1.25ml/¼ tsp ground nutmeg
1.25ml/¼ tsp ground cinnamon

1. Put all the dried fruit, orange rind and orange juice into a large bowl and mix well.

2. Put about half of the mixed fruit into the base of a lightly buttered ovenproof serving dish.

3. Spread the bread with the butter and cut it into small squares.

4. Arrange half of the bread squares over the fruit in the base of the serving dish.

5. Sprinkle with half of the brown sugar, then repeat the layers once again, finishing with a layer of sugar.

6. Whisk together the milk, eggs, nutmeg and cinnamon. Pour the mixture over the bread pudding and allow to stand for 1 hour.

7. Bake the pudding in a preheated oven, 190°C/375°F/ Gas Mark 5, for about 35-40 minutes, or until crisp on top but still soft at the bottom. Serve very hot.

Step 5 Arrange the fruit, bread and sugar in layers in an ovenproof dish.

Step 3 Cut the buttered bread into squares approximately 5cm/2 inches.

Step 6 Pour the egg and milk mixture over the bread and fruit, taking care not to dislodge the pieces of bread.

Cook's Notes

Time
Preparation takes 15 minutes, plus 1 hour soaking. Cooking takes 40 minutes.

Freezing
This pudding will freeze well and should be reheated for 20 minutes in a hot oven, 190°C/375°F/ Gas Mark 5. Cover the top with foil to prevent it from burning or browning further.

Vitamin Content
Dried fruit is an excellent source of vitamin C, and milk and eggs are good sources of vitamins A, B, D and E. Wholemeal bread is an excellent source of vitamins B and E.

SERVES 4
CARAMEL ORANGES

Rich in vitamins A and C, oranges need very little preparation to provide a delicious dessert.

4 large oranges
280g/10oz granulated sugar
340ml/12 fl oz water
60ml/2 fl oz boiling water
30ml/2 tbsps Cointreau

1. Using a potato peeler or very sharp knife, carefully pare the peel only from the oranges. Cut this peel into very thin strips, removing any white pith as you do so.

2. Put the orange peel strips into a small bowl and cover with boiling water. Allow to stand for 20 minutes, then drain.

3. Carefully peel all the pith from the oranges with a serrated edged knife. Cut the oranges horizontally into slices approximately 5ml/¼-inch thick. Reserve any juice which spills in a small jug.

4. Put the orange juice, the 340ml/12 fl oz water and sugar into a small saucepan, and heat gently all the time until the sugar has dissolved.

5. Increase the temperature and bring the sugar syrup to the boil, boiling rapidly until it turns a pale gold colour.

6. Remove the caramel from the heat and quickly stir in the 60ml/2 fl oz of boiling water.

7. Add the orange rind to the sugar syrup along with the Cointreau, and allow to cool completely.

8. Arrange the orange slices in a serving dish, and pour over the cooled syrup. Chill for several hours or overnight, before serving.

Step 1 Cut the parred orange rind into very thin julienne strips with a sharp knife.

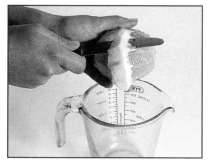

Step 3 Carefully remove all the white pith from the oranges, using a serrated knife and cutting with a sawing action.

Step 5 Cook the sugar and the syrup over a moderate heat, until it turns pale gold in colour. Take care not to overcook at this stage.

Cook's Notes

Time
Preparation takes 25 minutes, cooking takes 20 minutes.

Watchpoint
Take care not to overcook the sugar syrup or it will burn and spoil the flavour.

Preparation
Hold the pan slightly away from you when adding the boiling water, as the syrup will splutter and spit and can give a very nasty burn.

Freezing
Fresh oranges freeze very well, but sugar syrup should be made fresh each time.

Vitamin Content
Oranges are an excellent source of vitamins A and C.

MAKES 1 x 25cm/10-INCH LOAF

CARROT CAKE

Carrots give a cake a delicious sweet flavour, as well as lots of vitamins and minerals. What better excuse do you need to indulge in this delicious tea-time treat.

175g/6oz butter
175g/6oz soft brown sugar
2 eggs, well beaten
225g/8oz plain wholemeal flour
7.5ml/1½ tsps bicarbonate of soda
2.5ml/½ tsp baking powder
1.25ml/¼ tsp ground cinnamon
1.25ml/¼ tsp ground nutmeg
2.5ml/½ tsp salt
225g/8oz peeled carrots, grated
90g/3oz raisins
60g/2oz finely chopped walnuts
1.25ml/¼ tsp cardamom seeds, crushed
Icing sugar, for dredging

1. Cream the butter and sugar together until they are light and fluffy.

2. Add the eggs a little at a time, beating well and adding a teaspoonful of the flour with each addition, to prevent the mixture from curdling.

3. Put the remaining flour into a large bowl along with the bicarbonate of soda, baking powder, cinnamon, nutmeg and salt. Mix together well.

4. Carefully fold the flour into the butter and egg mixture, mixing well to ensure that it is blended evenly.

5. Add the carrots, raisins, nuts and cardamom seeds, beating the mixture well to blend evenly.

6. Lightly grease a 25cm/10-inch loaf tin and line the base with a piece of silicone paper.

7. Pour the cake mixture into the loaf tin, and bake in a preheated oven 180°C/350°F/Gas Mark 4, for 45-50 minutes or until a fine metal skewer comes out clean when inserted into the centre of the cake.

8. Cool the cake in its tin for 15 minutes before turning out onto a wire rack to cool completely.

9. Dredge the cake with icing sugar just before serving.

Step 2 Beat the eggs gradually into the butter and sugar, adding a little flour with each addition to prevent the mixture from curdling.

Step 5 Stir the carrots, fruit and nuts into the cake mixture, mixing well to blend evenly.

Cook's Notes

 Time
Preparation takes 30 minutes, cooking takes 45-50 minutes.

 Watchpoint
If the egg and butter mixture should curdle, add a little more flour and beat very hard with an electric whisk until the curdling disappears.

 Vitamin Content
Wholemeal flour is an excellent source of vitamins B and D. Carrots are an excellent source of vitamins A and C.

MAKES 1 x 20cm/8-INCH CAKE

TOASTED ALMOND CAKE

A crunchy toasted almond topping makes this cake very different from run-of-the-mill tea-time treats.

150g/5oz butter, softened
90g/3oz caster sugar
2 eggs, lightly beaten
180g/6oz wholemeal self-raising flour
2.5ml/½ tsp vanilla essence
30ml/2 tbsps orange juice
60g/2oz soft brown sugar
60ml/4 tbsps melted, unsalted, butter
15ml/1 tbsp milk
60g/2oz flaked almonds
60g/2oz icing sugar
30ml/2 tbsps cornflour
3 egg yolks
140ml/¼ pint milk
90ml/3 fl oz double cream, whipped
1.25ml/¼ tsp almond essence

1. Cream the butter and caster sugar until it is light and fluffy.

2. Beat in the eggs one at a time, adding a teaspoonful of the flour with each addition to prevent the mixture from curdling.

3. Fold in all the remaining flour, along with the vanilla essence and the orange juice.

4. Lightly grease a 20cm/8-inch cake tin, and line the base with a piece of silicone paper.

5. Spoon the cake mixture into the tin and spread the top evenly with a palette knife.

6. Put the brown sugar into a small saucepan, along with the melted butter, the 15ml/1 tbsp milk and the flaked almonds. Stir over a low heat until the sugar has completely dissolved.

7. Sprinkle about 15ml/1 tbsp of additional flour over the top of the cake mixture in the tin, then pour over the melted sugar, butter and almond mixture. Spread it evenly, but try not to disturb the cake mixture too much.

8. Bake the cake in a preheated oven 190°C/375°F/Gas Mark 5 for 20-30 minutes, or until the cake is well risen and the topping has caramelised golden brown.

9. Put the icing sugar, cornflour and egg yolks into a bowl, and using an electric beater, whisk until they are light and fluffy.

10. Pour on the milk, gradually whisking between additions. Strain this egg yolk mixture through a sieve into a heavy-based saucepan.

11. Cook the egg yolk and milk mixture over a gentle heat until it begins to thicken, and will thickly coat the back of a wooden spoon. Stir the mixture frequently during the cooking time to prevent it from burning or curdling.

12. Remove from the heat and cool.

13. When the custard is completely cool, lightly fold in the cream and the almond essence.

14. When the cake has cooled, carefully cut it in half horizontally with a sharp knife. Sandwich the two halves back together using the almond custard as a filling.

15. Chill thoroughly before serving.

Cook's Notes

Time
Preparation takes 40 minutes. Cooking takes about 30 minutes, plus 10 minutes for the filling.

Watchpoint
Do not allow the flaked almond topping to become too hot. Heat it just long enough to dissolve the sugar. If it does overheat, allow it to cool before pouring onto the uncooked cake mixture.

Vitamin Content
Wholemeal flour contains B group vitamins and vitamin E. Nuts contain vitamins B and E, and butter and eggs contain vitamins A, B, D and E. Milk and cream contain vitamins A and D.

MAKES 1 x 20cm/8-INCH CAKE

CINNAMON BUTTER CREAM CAKE

This sumptuous cake has the added advantage of requiring no cooking.

280g/10oz granulated sugar
2.5ml/½ tsp ground cinnamon
90ml/6 tbsps water
8 egg yolks
450g/1lb unsalted butter, softened
48 sponge fingers
120ml/8 tbsps brandy
120g/4oz toasted almonds, roughly chopped
120g/4oz plain chocolate, coarsely grated

Step 9 Line the cake tin with trimmed sponge biscuits spread with approximately half of the butter cream.

1. Put the sugar, water and cinnamon in a small heavy-based saucepan and bring to the boil, stirring constantly until the sugar dissolves.

2. Allow the sugar syrup to boil briskly without stirring, until it begins to thicken, but has not browned. This temperature should be 113°C/236°F on a sugar thermometer; or when the sugar mixture will form a small ball when dropped into a bowl of cold water

3. Beat the egg yolks in a large bowl with an electric mixer, until they are pale and thick.

4. Pour the sugar syrup quickly, in a thin steady stream, into the whisked egg yolks, beating constantly with the electric beater.

5. Continue beating in this way until the mixture is thick, smooth and creamy. Allow to cool at room temperature.

6. Still using the electric mixer, beat the softened butter a spoonful at a time, into the egg and sugar mixture. Whisk well to ensure that it is evenly distributed. Chill the mixture until it reaches spreading consistency.

7. Line a 20cm/8-inch square tin with greased foil or silicone paper.

8. Cut the sponge fingers into neat pieces to enable you to use them to line the cake tin.

9. Divide the butter cream in half and spread a little of the butter cream lightly on one side of each biscuit and place them, icing side down, into the tin.

10. Cut any small pieces of biscuits to fill any corners, if necessary.

11. Continue spreading the butter cream on the biscuits and lining the cake tin in this way, alternating the direction of the fingers between the layers.

12. Sprinkle half of the brandy over the sponge biscuits, then continue spreading the remainder of the sponge with just half of the butter cream and filling the cake tin completely. Sprinkle with the remaining brandy, then chill in the refrigerator overnight.

13. Remove the cake from the tin and peel off the paper or foil. Slide the cake onto a flat surface and coat with the remaining half of the butter cream.

14. Press the chopped almonds on to the sides of the cake and decorate the top with the grated chocolate. Serve immediately, or chill in the refrigerator until required.

Cook's Notes

Time
Preparation takes about 45 minutes, plus overnight chilling.

Freezing
This cake freezes well.

Variation
The icing may be flavoured with 10ml/2 tsps instant coffee powder, which should be added when making the syrup.

Vitamin Content
Butter contains vitamins A, B and D, and eggs contain vitamins B and E. Nuts contain vitamins B and E.

Index

COMPILED BY PATRICIA PAYNE
EDITED BY JILLIAN STEWART
PHOTOGRAPHY BY PETER BARRY
RECIPES STYLED BY HELEN BURDETT
DESIGNED BY TINA LEE
COVER DESIGN BY MARILYN O'NEONS